MAKING

AN

ANGEL

MAKING
AN
ANGEL

POEMS

by

WALTER

JAMES

MILLER

Library of Congress Cataloging in Publication Data

Miller, Walter James,
    Making an angel

    I. Title.
PS3563.I42148M3   811'.5'4   77-4747
ISBN 0-918524-01-6

Pylon Press Inc.
New York, New York

ACKNOWLEDGMENTS

"Making an Angel" and "Street Scene" have appeared in *New York Quarterly*; "Cliff Dwellers at Mesa Verde" and "A Rocky Mountain Cloud" in *Western Humanities Review*; "Noon Whistle" in *The New York Times*; "Baroque Concert," "Windy Moment on Brooklyn Heights," "By Any Other Name," "Morning at Camp," "Ceres Loathes us Everywhere," "Elpenor's Eloquence" in *Poet Lore*. An abridged version of *Joseph in the Pit* (copyright 1969, 1977) and several of the lyrics have been broadcast over WEVD Radio, WNYC-TV, WNYC-FM, WNYU-FM. Grateful acknowledgment is hereby made to all editors, publishers, and producers involved, but especially to Florence Becker Lennon, Miriam Andrews, and William Packard.

FOR BONNIE

and Lisa, Jared, Robin,
Jason, and Naomi

Poems are like children—
easy to sire and difficult to educate
                Robinson Jeffers

TRALFAMADORIAN FOREWORD

KURT VONNEGUT, JR.	I liked your poem.
WALTER JAMES MILLER	You did? I'm glad you understood it.
KURT VONNEGUT, JR.	Who said I understood it? I said I liked it.

CONTENTS

CLIFF DWELLERS
AT MESA VERDE

Into the cracks in the tableland
They tucked their pueblos, small adjustments
In the cliffline, nests of clay and stick.
Below the scorched mesa, embracing
The sandstone damp with sea memory,
They scooped out their cool cells for the drape
Of loosened limb, for the shape of love

They sketched their rooms in free hand: floors lift
Like strata, walls surprise like outcrops,
Bricks touch like spilled rocks that drifted
Into status. Here they hardly dreamed
Nightmares of the right angle, or schemed
The tautest distance between two points,
Or heard the pressures of perfect cubes.

BAROQUE CONCERT

Vowels ascend the down escalator
  And sweating sweetens the resin
As countertenors down centuries astound
  The corduroy acoustics and me

But even where architects fondle a cantata
  And microphones troll from time's bridge
I hear again my own obbligato
  Rising in the eagerslowed bassoon

Quintillions of flurry-tailed notes
  Swarm in upwarms, swim in sweet alarms
Toward a truer pitch, where my lover brackets
  Chaos into a chord

CERES LOATHES US EVERYWHERE

Frozen fractions, flicked from glaciers,
Floating nine-tenths under,
Dreams that navigate through sleep
Are doomed to slip
Beneath a golden Gulf Stream,
Known by the moment of waking
As only a sudden melting

I: civilian: cursed in the cursing
Of troops through history:
From the Hot Gates to the Zeroed-in-Wadi:
Crept to the damp edge of dawn
Sweat-and-dew wet
Helmet to helmet
In a whispering patrol
Tensed against
Another day's surprise:
Mistward the morning glowed
The sun rose a pointed sun

A brilliant cylinder shaping up familiar
A giant cannon-shell flung quiet
As breathing through the dawn's usual path
The ultimate in flares
Flattening out our day-dragged vigil:
We held the dark west where suns usually set

Segue a sudden melting
Of celluloid: home movies

But dreams that cruise in daylight
Like jeeps on parade
Brood sweet nostalgia for the future

Seated at azimuth in the saddle of legal fury
I must hope for all time's giving in our gun's pivot
I: civilian: swivel my crew
Twelve men track the zodiac
Impatient like boyish ambivalence
Thrusting with a gun-tube
Inside all of space but all of it
And even space itself receding
Gluteal squeezes in reverse
Impotent frets for the fatal focus:
O FIRE! FIRE! FIRE!
Unstitching across the pulse
Of any bombing bird's unfeathering

Out there too the sniper broods
On time when truth is not guerrilla
Firing furtive from a plugged foxhole
Nostalgia squeezes his trigger
Nostalgia turns our lathes somewhere
Nostalgia for the future
Fuels the flier's heart
Far far inland where his target
Screams surprise and vomits lava
Ceres loathes us everywhere

WINDY MOMENT ON BROOKLYN HEIGHTS

A billion sailsful of arrogant air,
Protean, flicked off alien floes, funneling
In from the harbor, cossacked and bravuraed
Up my street, glutted and shut my breath

A doorman, hotel's azure ornament,
Clutched for his poise; an idling chauffeur
(Cap commandeered around the corner, gone)
Sealed his Cadillac in glass and breathed himself

From an alley, as from wings of the ballet,
Rolled a push-cart glorious on course,
And pushed-pushing, knees rising as though racing
Over surf, ecstasy exploding
His shag moustache, the grocer's "boy" loped by,
Carib face afloat on waves of wind

MAKING AN ANGEL

So in love with suspense
  She laughs herself backwards
    Raccoonfur fuzzes out
      Amber charging snow
        Buoys the girl like lake
          Who floats flat still
            Eyes navigating blue
              Undrinking immersed

              And he vertical thinks
              Splinters in his heart
              Even she very verdure of rapture
              Could will stretch to cold white suspense

MORNING AT CAMP

In the dank capillaries
Of Lonelihood Forest,
This fern-floored brooding
Of soggy-barked limbs
And ghoulish knotholes,
I poke in squat grass,
I scrape limp termites
From wood once wood,
But nowhere do I find the dry twig
To light a lover's hope with

Wind runs rivers through the trees
Sunlight shivers in shy corners
A squirrel's journey
Is many short-lived squirrels
I cannot find the dry twig the hope

July two Julys parallel Julys
Two-line two-lie Julys that never intersect

April we have haunted rain
May aloofness sat enchanted on the rooftops
June lingered on thirty farewell corners
Always there were two Julys
Yours and mine

Evenings around the camp's eccentric fire
Day tightened to hard stars
Moons as sharp as Euclid
I think woodfires burn to the
Bursting core for
Lovered lovers only:
For the loving but loverless
The staring at scattered sounds
Footsteps on the mind
Shooting stars
Like pipe-sparks from some quiet smoker
Fled into the corner of the cornea
For the lonely (for the lorn
The word lorn is never *Obs.* never "corn")
For the lonely
Only the question
On the pillow in the morning

Now I hear the cook's shout above the bubbling bacon
From the hill where our tent has brought
Fulfillment to the unawakened curve:
And he will ask me where's the wood?
And I shall answer that
A camper's moods are weather
A lover's moods are distances
A poet's moods a poem's progress
And so on brooding
Billy boy I have you three to one

A ROCKY MOUNTAIN CLOUD

A Rocky Mountain cloud, white sails with dirty bilge,
Hints that a virile day can die of chill

A change a change of mind a chipmunk frets my fire
Waves his stripe adjusts his nose and tries his other
Eye and punctuates his questions with his tail

Beside beside himself: the stream slides out of the shade
And tilting to a satin glare, wigs over a boulder
And gloving and ungloving a root, ripples to a gel.

Unflurried, first collecting his tithe, a greycoat bird
Swerves for a crust and perches on my percolator
Preaching chigi whirr, chichi chidgi whirr whirr

An aspen titters among the solemn spruce, wind
Hints into the tent a day can die of chill
And lifts and lilts the blankets of my goldlint child

Who rouses when I leap up when an indignant grouse
Like a motorboat that shouts its startled starting
Flushes up and churns a tumult through the spruce

And drowsing down again my goldlint girl inhales a dream
But I I pulse the why of the grouse's plangent panic

I clock the gentle crush of moccasin on leaf
And heart lets loins acknowledge now these lush
Congeries of nameless heirs: verving toward Eve

UP? NO, DOWN

Up?

> She took a long long time
> to learn to kill time

No, down!

> erection? what's an erection!
> even my husband gets erections

> > fame came late
> > for him
> > fame came lame

Eleven out please!

> what's up?
> our tenth slowdown

Up?

No down

> the shell's a phallus
> the barrel's a vagina

This is nine?

> Mailer didn't say that
> one of his characters did

Four out please

> and so Rousseau became
> the first *artiste* in history
> to look a gift whore in the teats

Up?

> she told me, cousin,
> everything is relative, so

Negative!

> but she can't insist on incest

Fresh air at last

> all except maybe
> then again it's not

An up-and-down ride

> the story of my life
> from parasite to parricide

JOSEPH IN THE PIT

A Poem in Dialogue

THE ARGUMENT

There's something wrong with the Bible story of Joseph's encounter with his brothers at Dothan. Psychologically, esthetically, the scene seems incomplete, unsatisfying. This dramatic poem fills in the gaps and offers a new interpretation.

According to the traditional story, Joseph has infuriated his brothers by appearing before them in his new, aristocratic garb. They toss him into a cistern and plan to kill him. Reuben saves Joseph's life by proposing that they sell him into slavery instead.

This has the grave disadvantage of representing Joseph as nothing but a passive figure in the most critical hour of his life. But his earlier conduct suggests that he knows he has genius and can assert it boldly, and certainly his later behavior in Egypt proves he is able to take the initiative and exploit circumstances. Furthermore, the action at the pit is so profoundly symbolic

24

of Joseph's life that it must serve as a revelation, an inspiration to him. How much more artistic, then, to think of Joseph as seizing the Dothan confrontation as his opportunity himself to resolve the family impasse.

How? In this poem, partly by means of a third dream not reported in the Bible but akin to the two that are. Through this vision, in one stroke he proves his new maturity, to himself and to us. And so it is he himself who prevents his brothers from committing murder, he who saves his own life. Thus he also demonstrates his confidence that he can still rise to the top even if he must first descend to the bottom. He goes to Egypt as an act of will. He is not discovered there by Potiphar. He discovers himself before he goes there.

Joseph's resolution of the family dilemma through deliberate use of a third vision is completely in character, and it undoes the damage perpetrated by his earlier dreams: one assumption here is that Joseph, as part of his coming of age in the Dothan crisis, is deliberately reversing the effects of his earlier—immature—manifestations of genius.

How can all this be reconciled with the Bible account? Does it provide us with an interpretation more in harmony with modern concepts of character?

Joseph will tell

W J M

NOTES FOR TWO AUDIENCES

For *the reading audience*, I present the play as a poem. So that the reader may enjoy the flow of music and ideas without interruption, I offer no stage directions except the name of the speaker of the moment. The reader has no trouble, though, in visualizing the action: the speeches describe both scene and movement.

But for actors and directors planning for *the viewing-and-listening audience*, a few other directions are advisable. Speeches marked for CHORUS, or for a part of the chorus, e.g., SONS OF LEAH, should be spoken in unison only when the brothers stand solidly together, locked in conformity. At other times, choral speeches should be heard as conversations within that group, with different lines alternated, scattered, reinforced as the director sees fit.

Although there are twelve speaking parts, there need be only half that number of actors. The illusion of ten brothers is easily created by having four or five actors moving near, and grouping and regrouping with, five or six figures painted on flats. The painted figures wear the same "purple of people" as the live figures wear. Only Reuben, among the ten older brothers, needs a slightly different costume—maybe he wears a head-band. Four or five voices suffice to carry all the parts, while the painted figures reinforce the impression of the brothers' stolid immobility. One of the brothers sent to summon the Karawan Bashi can, after a change of costume, return *as* the Bashi.

The poetry will also suggest to the director numerous possibilities for choreographic movement, posturings, groupings; for grotesque lighting effects; for bizarre tableaux of Joseph in the Pit (which could be seen in cross-section) and Reuben "on the rim," the caravan on the "double horizon," and so on.

W J M

DRAMATIS PERSONAE

CHORUS OF JOSEPH'S TEN OLDER BROTHERS:

Reuben	)	
Simeon	)	
Judah	)	Jacob's Sons
Issachar	)	by Leah
Levi	)	
Zebulon	)	
Dan	)	Jacob's Sons
Naphtali	)	by Rachel's Bilhah
Gad	)	Jacob's Sons
Asher	)	by Leah's Zilpah

JOSEPH   Jacob's Son by Rachel, the favorite wife

KARAWAN BASHI   Headman of the caravan

JOSEPH IN THE PIT

SONS BY BILHAH

I want always to answer to the same name.
Sand grains should shift slow as brown sheep brown goats drift
From grasses to grasses, green pasture past the next
Green like the last, each green chew a taste retasted.
Change should nibble its way, change should ruminate,
Change renew renewal, as seasons change places

SONS BY ZILPAH

I know a blistering river of wind will simmer out.
Wadi, gash of a flash flood, contains and drains.
Stars ride wide but their patterns are unstirred.
I want always to be called by the same name

SONS BY LEAH

When sharp stars ride in pride within the pull of pattern
When caravans meander but unravel sacred routes
When breathing awe of orbits I follow grasses greening
Then heart sits by its own hearth, then honey glows gold
Honey at the table, in the bed, glows sweet serene
O heart always answer to the same name

REUBEN

I agree in chorus, disagree in soliloquy.
Reuben's ambition is unleavened with courage.
Father disturbed the stars with a dish of red lentils.
Born with a birthwrong, he cooked himself the birthright
Born with a birthwrong, Jacob set it right

CHORUS

I know a

REUBEN

Looking up at Esau, he seesawed him down
Spawned the bottom son, he sired himself the top one

CHORUS

blistering river

REUBEN

Brothers for whom brown sheep glow brown goats glow forget
Jacob bred speckled goats, his black sheep heckled the stars

CHORUS

of wind is

REUBEN

Jacob flared like a hot sirocco out of season.
Who blazed your sacred routes from grazing to grazing?

CHORUS

simmering out

REUBEN

Embraced by divine muscle, he tasted angel sweat
And wrestling without rest, Jacob changed his name

SONS BY LEAH

Serenity!

SONS BY BILHAH

Amenity!

SONS BY ZILPAH

Identity!
I want forever to answer to the same name

REUBEN

Jacob wrestled, ten sons rest; father flamed, sons glow

CHORUS

Serenity! Amenities!

REUBEN

Nonentities!
No I flamed briefly once Reuben flamed in chief's wife
Tasted fierce vermilion, shade of Jacob's rebellion
Jacob shaped his own couch, Reuben flamed in father's couch

CHORUS

Impatient with last night's stars, hasting strangers chafe
All valleys look alike in chains of Canaan hills.
They chase gauche comets. Herd-braced, brooding, I know
Each acacia differs gracious, each star's a different face
Each gesture that I know is a long language of love

SONS BY LEAH

On greyrock ridge—against bleachfading sky!
A meteor, cooling blue in daylight?

DAN

A striped sail!

LEVI

Drifting overland?

GAD

Bush bursting alien blooms.

ZEBULON

A children's rainbow?

ASHER

Slowed and slurred visions
Of sun digesting in my goldshot eye.

JUDAH

Branches, leaves on fire?

ASHER

No, limbs in flaming sleeves
A prince in linen tunic!

ISSACHAR

Alone?

NAPHTALI

A god then

REUBEN

Steward looking crew-ward. Man seeks his men

SONS BY LEAH

I wear solid purple

SONS BY ZILPAH

Sleeves muffle work

SONS BY BILHAH

I wear purple wool of populace

SONS BY LEAH

I wear sleeveless wool of people

SONS BY BILHAH

Wool drenched in grape, dye cinched with dung of goat

CHORUS

Not *his* purple shade: for *his* purple red
Someone dredged a knuckled whelk, unsnailed a snail
For his breezy yellow, squeezed an almond leaf
For crimson, bled and bladdered a madder root
For violet blue, violated through
To inner indigo secrets of peas
For pitch patch, sucked stark pomegranate bark
That tunic paled the sea paled the soil

ZEBULON

I know that careful-careless drift-wing-drift
Walk that's like his talk, a floating lift

SONS BY BILHAH

Tattler!

SONS BY ZILPAH

Dreamer!

SONS BY LEAH

And eleventh son,
Dressed like a sundrenched cloud at sunrest!

JUDAH

My father drapes me in grape-drenched woolen
And dredges snails to dye that telltale's linen?
Father is the lamb greater than the ram?
Father is the twig bigger than the limb?

33

REUBEN

Joseph grew in a grove of ten grown brothers
Sapling seeking light beyond a taller bole and branch
Look up, his shed leaves are falling, fall on us

CHORUS

Steward looking crew-ward—boy seeking men!

DAN

Come to catch us in our slack satisfaction!

ASHER

What, a ram not jumping, ramming, pumping?

CHORUS

Joseph will tell!

NAPHTALI

What, a man not pimping for his unused ewes?

CHORUS

Joseph will tell!

GAD

Yes a lamb strayed while I played in love's cave

CHORUS

Joseph will tell!

JUDAH

Unless he dazedreams over a dayglazed nightmare
Oh his daymares fretbeget my nightfrightmares

SONS BY ZILPAH

While we found and bound: embraced with twenty biceps:
Ten arm-around sheaves, stalks soaking chesty sweat,
He found and bound none

SONS BY LEAH

Yet in his gazegleam dazedream
Ten sheaves shiverbowed before one sheaf ungatherbound!

SONS BY BILHAH

While ten brothers swingleaped in dance for chief and chief wife,
Flinging spine from finger, kissing breasty brine,
He danced standing still

SONS BY LEAH

And in his fancy trance
Ten stars, moon and sun, pulled in pattern, paled before his
comet glare

SIMEON

He levels down as if that ridge is heaven's stair

CHORUS

Fall on us! Blacken grass but blaze to core, meteor boy!
Simmer out, blistering wind! Drain away, flash flood

REUBEN

Unleavened with courage, Reuben disagrees in soliloquy:
Filigree revision: his vision's our condition

JOSEPH'S VOICE

Brothers do you know me?

SIMEON

Do glow-worms glow?

JOSEPH'S VOICE

Brothers do you hear me?

LEVI

Do earwigs fear prigs?

JUDAH

In slack satisfaction I snatch at a fast vision:
Joseph's in oblivion, his coat is simple crimson

CHORUS

His tunic won't illuminate the gorgeous day?
No memory of sun splurging in goldshot eye?

JUDAH

Tell father a lion violated the violet
Squeezed the breezy yellow uncometed the comet
Father, Joseph bled and dyed his tunic simple red

CHORUS

Finished in sleeveless linen: sleeveless seamless dreamless

REUBEN

Before this sudden brotherscud floods out the flame with blood
Can Reuben's love bank the fire, huddlehoard the flame?
Cease whispering in solo, cease whispering in chorus.
Listen brothers do not bleed the glistening brother
Smother his visions: imprison the glisten in the cistern!

JOSEPH

Brothers rejoice, Joseph speaks with Jacob's voice.

SONS OF ZILPAH

Rip the panic tunic! Strip the unique eunuch!

SONS OF BILHAH

Peel the tulip petals! Mealy flesh! Peel the purple red—
maggot muscle!

SONS BY LEAH

Ah you frail travesty on my male majesty
Drop deep in drab dream. Glisten in cistern, sister

ISSACHAR

Ah the passion passed too fast, exhausted with no tall climb

SIMEON

In the limp grass the wind still prowls

LEVI

Should the arrow leave the archer quivering like his bowstring?

ZEBULON

If only I could hoist a sail on the boat of our boasting

SIMEON

wind still drifts

SONS BY BILHAH

Horizon glides subsides, wadi contains and drains
No bush is flaming alien blooms
No striped sail floats boatless. Acacias blaze gracious
Hunter follows hind, shepherd hallows grazing
Heart sits by its own hearth when stars stride in orbit pride

REUBEN

Find and bind the pieces, peace ungatherbound

CHORUS

Serenity is amenity is intensity
I want forever to answer to the same name

JOSEPH'S VOICE

Brothers pioneers of my being, trying ears trying eyes for
        trailing brother
Reuben who churned and sieved all his years' alternatives for
        trailing brother
Issachar who guarded the outside stars so I could dream inside
        the night
Judah who knew the path who was my feet so I could stare above
        beyond away

Brothers if remembering this hour locust-crowds your eyes,
wolf-cloys your ears
Sets fires to your sleep, Oh do not hug remorse, Oh do not
whore on guilt's chafed belly

SONS BY BILHAH

When we store grain in cistern pit we know what for
Sheaf ungatherbound is stored underground. What for?

JOSEPH

You raise your coat you batter your sandals
To outrace the knuckled reach of rockslide

CHORUS

Change should ruminate

JOSEPH

Platitudinous you had to do this
Turtle must blink at alien shadow
Shrink his world inside his shoulder overhead

CHORUS

change renew renewal

JOSEPH

You could not stare into my comet glare
You could not live behind vermilion lids
In leaden light you shed on each other
Each brother must see himself in brother

CHORUS

Easy gaze of brother ways he leans into his days
Each gesture that I know is a long language of love

JOSEPH

Thigh of hating, thigh of loving, stride
Together, swinging high the seed of seed

38

REUBEN

Joseph sapling in grove of grown brothers

JOSEPH

Reuben who turned and sieved his lost alternatives

REUBEN

This is no blessed jest . . .

CHORUS

Fretbeget nightfrightmares

REUBEN

. . . at a sheepshearing feast

CHORUS

digest in goldshut eye

REUBEN

Judah broods a sacrifice . . .

CHORUS

Purple wool of populace

REUBEN

. . . falters only at what altar

CHORUS

sleeves murder work

REUBEN

To slit you on . . .

CHORUS

Lion-violated

REUBEN

. . . which ritual . . .

CHORUS

uncometed

REUBEN

. . . to hit you with

CHORUS

solid red

REUBEN

But smooth each knuckle of their truculence
Glut their mood with succulent nostalgia
For trailing youngling while I barter for succor
In far oasis in forest in far bazaar

JOSEPH

You show the gloss yet know the dross

REUBEN

The dross is?

JOSEPH

The farther the forest the smaller the horrors
For brother courageous in solo, coward in chorus

REUBEN

Starfish dredged from darkness

JOSEPH

Reuben whose derision is unleavened with courage

REUBEN

stretchdries in sun

JOSEPH

Sired the first boy you spawned yourself the last

REUBEN

And bleaches to socket

JOSEPH

O Reuben even if I do stab true, candor can do as vilely as vice
When it's aimed to stun not stir, to bleed not feed
Candor that shoves instead of loves is pious bias

REUBEN

blisters vermilion

JOSEPH

Still whose elbowing is it that I'm a critic at an elbow
a chilling chider
Ribber nibbling at his siblings' shibboleths?

REUBEN

Eleventh boyframe sprung from Jacob's lust
But first boyface born of his love
Not spilled like us in the fast hutch of eyeless concubinage
But sired in the long palace of eye-in-eye desire
Rachel saved you for last like ladling the gravy
Jacob gapes at you the way when bathing away
Six sweaty days he gapes into the Sabbath

JOSEPH

Never have I shivered at the stars with Naphtali in the nights
of hard herding
But I jollied at the shearing of the sheep
Never have I sweat with Zebulon in the starved zest of sowing
But I ravished the harvest

REUBEN

and you relish a starred vest
Rachel saved you for last when bathing away
Six sweating days Jacob could savor a sweet Sabbath

41

JOSEPH

Afraid when you threw me eschewed me
Arrayed in nudeness you made me
Steward of our brooding
Amused steward of views of us
You evaded and eluded

SIMEON

Double horizon on greyrock ridge!

SONS BY ZILPAH

Camel and man
Camel and man
       and camel
       and

SONS BY LEAH

   Caravan
Filing whiling
To the Nile
Humping hunching
Bumping bunching
Caterpillar crawling

SONS BY ZILPAH

Camels meander
But caravan unravels
Sacred ways
Of sacred days
In caterpillar crawl

JOSEPH

Down into the lone pit and up into my own wit
Flung they thought into earth's shit but slung I knew at a
              cloud's tit

SIMEON

Double horizon against bleachfading sky!

SONS BY BILHAH

Camels hunching
Bunching humping
Plodding daintily
Shoddily quaint
Their hope in hair-rope
From ass to camel
Camel ass to ass face

SONS BY ZILPAH

Grope hope mope hope
Following an air-rope
From camel to camel

SONS BY LEAH

Hallowing an heir's rope
From hamlet to hamlet
Caterpillar will

JOSEPH

Phlegmflung into pit far from hem of family
Spat out like the pit of an olive which planted and all-loved
Could have polished the salad with oil of the Of-all

SIMEON

Leader looms down heaven's stair

SONS BY LEAH

Spurting purple plumes
Plodding daintily

SONS BY BILHAH

Sprinkling yellow bells
Stolidly saintly

SONS BY ZILPAH

Brash with crimson sash
Shoddily quaint

Trailing tassels
Flailing assbells

SONS BY LEAH

Slowing slurring
Suns
Digesting in
My goldshot eye

SONS BY BILHAH

Careful caterpillar
In willynilly crawl
Larval traveler
Filing to the Nile

JOSEPH

Critic in the pit fall, cricket in the nightfall
Critic in the all-pit I always sit and watch and hatch
As all dribbling siblings bibbing cousins inlaws outlaws
Bibulously blur then blend into a blind band
Encamped on a shoutaway slope in a hillaway valley
What must be their hands shy at the fire
Limbs and torsos but no fingers or faces
For tossed so in pit I can know mankind but can know no man

CHORUS
Camels meander but caravans unravel

SONS BY BILHAH

Ample camels
Trampling gravel
Sampling sand
Heaving camphor
Balsam and fur
From shoulder to shoulder

SONS BY ZILPAH

Ceramics and myrrh

Charlatans artisans
Talismans courtesans
Dromedaries manned
Bactrians meandering
Dragging by hair-rope
Slaves to stave in
Slaves to grope in
Slaves for mud and stud
Slaves to lave in

JOSEPH

Crickets in the nightfall

SONS BY LEAH

Bactrians meandering
Caterpillar willing
Larval marvel
Willynilly careful
Whiling to the Nile
Niling a while

JOSEPH

Always brothers I want to be called by a new name

JUDAH

In our slack satisfaction where's our vision vanished
Of Joseph in oblivion, tunic drenched in crimson?

JOSEPH

Not bracing for a blistering wind but riding it

SONS BY BILHAH

Tell father a lion leaned on the yellow tulip

JOSEPH

Brothers born with a birthwrong let me cook you your birthright

SONS BY ZILPAH

Oh he's dancing standing still

JOSEPH

Brothers born with a birthwrong let me set it right

SONS BY LEAH

he's in his fancy trance

JOSEPH

Behold I have dazedreamed another daymare:
Eleven brothers peeled a field at Dothan
Found and severed stalks, bound eleven sheaves
Ten brothers stood aside astonisheyed
Ten sheaves stood purple-plain like perfect persons
One sheaf glowed
        indigo-yellow-crimson-alien violet
            like a rainbow princeling!
Asher-sheaf stalked to slash the Joseph-sheaf
In half and halves of halves but Reuben-sheaf
Shrewdly bleated: Don't bleed our brief chief
But sell our sheafling to Arab caravan
Oh carry our sheaf of clipped grief to Egypt!

SONS BY ZILPAH

Ten . . . purple plain . . . . like perfect persons?

SONS BY BILHAH

One . . . indiglowed . . . like a rainbow princeling?

REUBEN

Sell our chiefling to the Arab caravan
To carry our clipped grief to Egypt!

SONS BY BILHAH

O Reuben prudent improver of drab dreams!

46

SONS BY ZILPAH
Oh blistering dilemma is simmering out!

REUBEN
Filigree revision: his vision's our condition.
Asher, Dan, challenge the Karawan Bashi to a haggle

SONS BY BILHAH
O Reuben prudent improver of a drab dream

REUBEN
Oh Reuben's love will huddlehoard the flame

JOSEPH
O Reuben brother
Prudent improver
Would never discover
I was paddling
My gills away
Shedding a paddle
To shed a puddle
Hefting a lung
On a lunge
To taste dry day

ASHER
Camel and man
Camels and men
Random in tandem
Careful-careless drift
From hamlet to hamlet
To caravanserai
Karawan Bashi
Is ambling over

JOSEPH
Reuben brother
Prudent improver

47

Of drab dreams
Larval marvel
Nudest caterpillar
Willing always
To will himself no wings
No jeweling wings
No wings at all

KARAWAN BASHI
Eleven pieces of silver

SONS BY BILHAH
Eleven only?

KARAWAN BASHI
No muscles at all!

SONS BY ZILPAH
Muscles for telling!

KARAWAN BASHI
For telling?

SONS BY LEAH
Maybe a ram's not jumping ramming pumping?

KARAWAN BASHI
They're usually at it

SONS BY LEAH
But Joseph will tell!
A man's not pimping for his unused ewes?

KARAWAN BASHI
They're ewes-ually at it

CHORUS
But Joseph will tell!
A lamb strays while a slave plays in love's cave?

48

KARAWAN BASHI

They're always at it!

CHORUS

And Joseph will tattle!

JOSEPH

You raised your coat, you battered your sandals
To outrace the knuckled reach of rockslide
Why should you rut now in guilt's dry cunt?

KARAWAN BASHI

Fifteen pieces of silver

SONS BY BILHAH

Steward looking crew-ward

JOSEPH

Platitudinous you had to do this
Turtle must blink at alien shadow
Shrink his world inside his shoulder

SONS BY ZILPAH

Catches them in their slack never turns his back

JOSEPH

You could not stand my comet glare
You could not live behind vermilion lids
In leaden light you shed on each other
Each brother must see himself in brother

KARAWAN BASHI

Twenty silver pieces: two to each other

SONS BY LEAH

Up you frail travesty on my male majesty
Tattler! Dreamer! And eleventh son

KARAWAN BASHI

Take off that linen loin-cloth put on a wool one

CHORUS

Undress those moons caressed with pink clouds

JOSEPH

Thigh of hating, thigh of mating, stride
Together swinging high the seed of seed

SONS BY BILHAH

Stars stride wide but their patterns are unstirred
Sand grains shift slow as brown sheep brown goats drift
From grasses to grasses, green pastures past the next
Green like the last, each green chew a taste retasted
Change should nibble its way change should ruminate
Change renew renewal as seasons change places

REUBEN

Reuben flared like a hot sirocco out of season

SONS BY ZILPAH

I know a blistering river of wind will simmer out
Wadi gash of a flash flood contains and drains

KARAWAN BASHI

My usual
Consumes your unusual

JOSEPH

Tadpole to toad
Is pond to dry wood
Caterpillar to butterfly
Is hole to sky
Tadpole good
        bye
Caterpillar good
        bye

50

SONS BY LEAH

When caravans meander but unravel sacred routes
And breathing awe of orbits I follow grasses greening
And heart sits by its own hearth then honey glows gold
Honey at the table in the bed glows sweet serene
O heart always always answer to the same name

JOSEPH'S VOICE

Brothers will you know me

SONS BY ZILPAH

Hasting strangers chafe
All valleys look alike in chains of Canaan hills

JOSEPH'S VOICE

know my new name?

CHORUS

They chase gauche comets. Herd-based, brooding, I know
Each acacia differs gracious, each star's a different face
Easy gaze of brother ways he leans into his days
Each gesture that I know is a long language of love

BY ANY OTHER NAME

A pudgy tug is nudging her.
The M/S *Imyaku* swells against her dock,
A swerve of indigo beneath a ziggurat of deck.

The tug is blazing orange, tires bubbling black
Along her gunwhales. She proclaims herself
The *Sidney Sweeter* in flaming italics
That crown the pilot house. She pulls away,
Insouciant center of a moving navel
On the smooth belly of the bay.

And who, you wonder, is Sidney Sweeter?
Oh Sidney he blinks at ocean spray
Oh Sidney blossoms in steam heat
Sidney gapes at bosoms never nudges buttocks
He plays with Sidney beneath his crackling sheets

IF OGDEN NASH WERE HERE, HE'D SAY

She's in her latency
Which means we have to wait and see

NOON WHISTLE

Now they have nosed the last poised girder
To permanence, relaxed the nervous crane
And stopped the stubborn tractor. Now
The hot singing shuddering rivets are cold
The glad artillery of engineers is calm.
Up through the rooms outlined in space
The steel stairways ascend the open day.
And knee-clinging cable-swinging down
From their hammered iron oath that squared
The air, from their forest of steel trunks sprung
From a barren lot, descend the casual men,
The average heroes of their time.

STREET SCENE

He raises the blind to smell the evening.
Question-marks hunch up in ten-watt doorways.
At the corner, frantic laughs
Clash like cymbals, vanish fast
In silent suction. Women are leaning
From windows of the day's fierce constriction,
Waiting for sleep to blur the angles
Of the kitchen. Lovers are looking
For a different lane down the same street.

He dreams of Frost as Two Frosts in Mud Time.
          What can I do? I cannot dangle like a kid
          Along the docks and sigh my future
          Toward the yachts and matronly riverboats.
          No flock of feathers and beaks ever migrates
          To my geranium to flaunt
          Some flippant descant. Sometimes I hear
          A cricket scrape its limited instrument.

He fades from the life-size window.
He finds—in the slow glowing of the tube—
His own two eyes made one and magnified.

ANTI-BALLAD

I was eleven
I was tall and straight
Like a
        b
        o
        w
        i
        e

        k
        n
        i
        f
        e

              in my walk
Along a street of beeches
As manicured
As the Age of Reason

She was sifting her own mist
Grey bone
Twisting a cobweb shawl . . .
To a green-banana boyman
She seemed a hundred and four

Fury banal as harpies
Shaped a sudden lip
In a brittling skull
She hated out a day-long spit:

"S
      N
            A
                  K
                        E
                              !"

Brownblack bruises would relax
The tight yellow banana
Twice eleven
Would know what she meant

But O my knifehood
Sheathed in cobweb
When would she?

WITH SOUL SO DEAD

What must be
A horizontal me
Barrels over the bed
Verges to vertical
The alarm clock
Ripping out the stitches
Of the night
Before I save
A thread a bit of lint

The ceiling is
Snowing letters
Letters from
Addressed to
Delivered all around

Deep in drifts
Stamps not pasted in the upper
Right-hand corner
But flaking off the envelopes
Flags and flurries
Gonfalons
Gone falling
Is the addressee
No better nor less
Than addressor
Is my signature
My dear sir?

Letters drift beside behind me
Maybe signed maybe sealed
Still unpeeled

Letters were they keys
To are these fetters I feel
Not that I can see
Letters splotch the floor
Before I punch
The duodecimal face
Into staccato quiet
And genuflect to pick them up
Letters melt in the varnish
Felt they vanish to
(Canst fade in the plaster
So fast, old mole?)
Where? Returned to sender,
Lender of my gender?
No return address
No forwarding
Dead letter office?
Where do civil servants
Shovel snowdrifts
Stamped
"Insufficient Postage"

I yawn out north south
Reach stretch east west
For a zip code, my new address
A map with an arrow:
You are here!

Breathing dutiful
With soul so dead
Always to myself I said it
Confessing now yes
This is my own, my latent
I begin to forget what
Was it youth in Asia
A mercy death?
I have not heard
Not a letter not a line
From myself since . . .
Was it . . . once
The androgen bath?
Or blizzards before that?

ELPENOR'S ELOQUENCE

Waiting for the dial tone
I hear a voice instead

      Wasn't Homer unkind
      Letting it stand that Elpenor
      "Not very valiant in war"
      Was vague in mind?

      When Elpenor fell
      From the topmost lintel
      Into the cool center
      Of the Circean circle,
      No one noticed

61

In the sizzle of official business
No one missed his silence.
Their conditioning of course
No one dined Demodokos
Or feted Phemios
To celebrate the quiet

Elpenor's "dramatic moment"
—When he rises like a dead minnow
In the bucket of my memory—
Yes Elpenor's eloquence
Came only when he pleaded
For decent interment.
The least they could do
Since at last he was feeling
Like everyone else

Three or four orbits behind us
I fell and died
And since the flattened
Cannot shovel themselves
And since the upright
Tried only to convince me
It hadn't happened
I putrefied
In the graveless air
Where upright people
Keep on trying
Mouth-to-mouth resuscitation
Osculation drags away my lips
And fillets my cheeks
Like lazy pirhanas
No one notices
A face has fallen open
And feeds on cheesy toes
No one

Only the dial tone is there

*Printed May 1977 by Edwards Brothers Inc., Ann
Arbor, Michigan. Typeset by Lambrecht
Typography & Design in Century Schoolbook.
Designed by Abigail Moseley.*

PYLON PRESS TITLES

Kurt Vonnegut, Jr: VONNEGUT TALKS with Walter James Miller about Writers and Writing (edited by Michael Chernuchin)

William Packard: FIRST SELECTED POEMS

Elizabeth Sargent: A Portrait of the Artist as A WOMAN IN LOVE; a novel

Walter James Miller: MAKING AN ANGEL

FORTHCOMING:

Jules Verne: EDGAR POE AND HIS WORKS (Translated by Eunice McAuley)

Stan Isaacs: STAN ISAACS' BEST; Collection of Literary Essays from *Newsday*